Getting the Right Fit: The Governing Board's Role in Hiring a Manager

Vaughn Mamlin Upshaw, John A. Rible IV, and Carl W. Stenberg

UNC
SCHOOL OF
GOVERNMENT

About the Series

Local Government Board Builders offers local elected leaders practical advice on how to effectively lead and govern. Each of the booklets in this series provides a topic overview, specific tips on effective practice, and worksheets and reflection questions to help local elected leaders improve their work. The series focuses on common activities for local governing boards, such as selecting and appointing committees and advisory boards, planning for the future, making better decisions, improving board accountability, and effectively engaging stakeholders in public decisions.

Vaughn Mamlin Upshaw, lecturer in public administration and government at the UNC School of Government, is the series editor.

Other Books in the Series

Leading Your Governing Board: A Guide for Mayors and County Board Chairs, Vaughn Mamlin Upshaw, 2009

A Model Code of Ethics for North Carolina Local Elected Officials, A. Fleming Bell, II, 2010

Creating and Maintaining Effective Local Government Citizen Advisory Committees, Vaughn Mamlin Upshaw, 2010

Working with Nonprofit Organizations, Margaret Henderson, Lydian Altman, Suzanne Julian, Gordon P. Whitaker, Eileen R. Youens, 2010

Public Outreach and Participation, John B. Stephens, Ricardo S. Morse, and Kelley T. O'Brien, 2011

Local Government Revenue Sources in North Carolina, Kara A. Millonzi, 2011

The School of Government at the University of North Carolina at Chapel Hill works to improve the lives of North Carolinians by engaging in practical scholarship that helps public officials and citizens understand and improve state and local government. Established in 1931 as the Institute of Government, the School provides educational, advisory, and research services for state and local governments. The School of Government is also home to a nationally ranked graduate program in public administration and specialized centers focused on information technology, environmental finance, and civic education for youth.

As the largest university-based local government training, advisory, and research organization in the United States, the School of Government offers up to 200 courses, seminars, and specialized conferences for more than 12,000 public officials each year. In addition, faculty members annually publish approximately fifty books, book chapters, bulletins, and other reference works related to state and local government. Each day that the General Assembly is in session, the School produces the *Daily Bulletin*, which reports on the day's activities for members of the legislature and others who need to follow the course of legislation.

The Master of Public Administration Program is a full-time, two-year program that serves up to sixty students annually. It consistently ranks among the best public administration graduate programs in the country, particularly in city management. With courses ranging from public policy analysis to ethics and management, the program educates leaders for local, state, and federal governments and nonprofit organizations.

Operating support for the School of Government's programs and activities comes from many sources, including state appropriations, local government membership dues, private contributions, publication sales, course fees, and service contracts. Visit www.sog.unc.edu or call 919.966.5381 for more information on the School's courses, publications, programs, and services.

Michael R. Smith, DEAN
Thomas H. Thornburg, SENIOR ASSOCIATE DEAN
Frayda S. Bluestein, ASSOCIATE DEAN FOR FACULTY DEVELOPMENT
Todd A. Nicolet, ASSOCIATE DEAN FOR OPERATIONS
Ann Cary Simpson, ASSOCIATE DEAN FOR DEVELOPMENT
Bradley G. Volk, ASSOCIATE DEAN FOR ADMINISTRATION

FACULTY

Gregory S. Allison	Alyson A. Grine	Christopher B. McLaughlin	Jessica Smith
David N. Ammons	Norma Houston	Laurie L. Mesibov	Karl W. Smith
Ann M. Anderson	Cheryl Daniels Howell	Kara A. Millonzi	Carl W. Stenberg III
A. Fleming Bell, II	Jeffrey A. Hughes	Jill D. Moore	John B. Stephens
Maureen M. Berner	Willow S. Jacobson	Jonathan Q. Morgan	Charles Szypszak
Mark F. Botts	Robert P. Joyce	Ricardo S. Morse	Shannon H. Tufts
Michael Crowell	Kenneth L. Joyner	C. Tyler Mulligan	Vaughn Upshaw
Shea Riggsbee Denning	Diane M. Juffras	David W. Owens	Aimee N. Wall
James C. Drennan	Dona G. Lewandowski	William C. Rivenbark	Jeffrey B. Welty
Richard D. Ducker	James M. Markham	Dale J. Roenigk	Richard B. Whisnant
Joseph S. Ferrell	Janet Mason	John Rubin	Gordon P. Whitaker

Printed in the United States of America

21 20 19 18 17   3 4 5 6 7

ISBN 978-1-56011-675-2

Contents

Introduction

Hiring a manager may be the most important decision a local governing board makes. The city or county manager is appointed by and works directly for the governing board, carrying out the board's policies, directing the local government organization, and representing the city or county in a variety of settings. A public manager has a substantial role in all aspects of local government and community affairs.

Experienced city and county managers were asked to provide feedback on their most and least successful hiring experiences and to offer suggestions for the hiring process. Excerpts from their responses appear throughout the book.

North Carolina is known as a "good government" state. This reputation is based in large part on the state's long history of using professional local government managers. Although the North Carolina General Statutes do not mandate that city and county governments hire managers, all of the state's one hundred counties and the majority of cities and towns with populations over five thousand have professional managers.

As North Carolina's population increases, more and more jurisdictions are seeking to hire managers. At the same time, many of the state's present managers are nearing retirement age. Local elected officials hoping to recruit and retain talented professional managers often face challenges as they identify and hire qualified candidates.

The governing board as a whole is responsible for selecting a public manager for the local government. To make sure the new manager will be a good fit for the organization, the board needs to agree on expectations for the new manager and design a process that will enable it to hire the best candidate for the job. Appendix 1 provides a list of eight expectations for effective board–manager relations.

Any board hiring a manager must first assume ownership of the process and recognize that it will probably be the most important decision they will make as a group. While the process may require some professional guidance and assistance, the board should remain involved in every phase of the selection process.

Getting the right fit rarely happens by accident. The chapters that follow provide local elected officials with an overview of their responsibilities in hiring a public manager and outline the essential steps in a successful hiring process.

The Manager's Role and Responsibilities

In North Carolina, a county board of commissioners or city council is legally responsible for organizing local government to promote the effective administration of government affairs.[1] Under the council–manager or board–manager (also known as the commission–manager) form of government, an elected board's policies are implemented by a manager who is appointed by the board. The manager is expected to carry out the board's directives efficiently, effectively, and equitably. As trusted advisors to their governing boards, managers also participate in policy development, providing regular reports on issues important to the organization and recommending measures considered expedient concerning operations.[2]

Municipalities

North Carolina's municipal boards have the option of operating under the mayor–council or the council–manager form of government. Smaller jurisdictions are more likely to operate under the mayor–council form, hiring staff to carry out day-to-day operations but assigning council members or council committees the responsibilities of overseeing one or more departments. Under the mayor–council form, a municipality can hire an administrator to provide oversight of the local government, and the council can decide how much or how little authority to delegate to the administrator. A council may—by policy or ordinance, for example—assign to the administrator responsibility for hiring, supervising, and firing all or some employees. Alternatively, municipal boards may legally adopt a council–manager form of government, giving all administrative responsibilities to the manager. By statute, under this form of government the manager is responsible for the day-to-day operations of the municipal government and hires and fires all personnel.[3]

---

1. See Sections 153A-76 and 160A-146 of the North Carolina General Statutes (hereinafter G.S.) for the specific authority granted to counties and municipalities, respectively.
2. G.S. 160A-148.
3. G.S. 160A-147.

In all but a few jurisdictions with special exceptions from the General Assembly, the council–manager form clearly delineates the responsibilities of the board and the manager, eliminating the option of any council member serving, even on an interim basis, as the public manager.

Counties

All one hundred counties in North Carolina operate under the board–manager form of government. By statute, a county board of commissioners may appoint a manager to oversee county government. Unlike a municipal council, however, a county board of commissioners may retain authority for hiring (or approving the hiring of) department heads. Another difference is that the board of commissioners may assign one of its members to serve as the county manager.

Statutory Roles and Responsibilities of Elected Officials and Public Managers

The distinct and complementary statutory roles of elected board members and public managers are set forth in Tables 1 and 2, below. Note, however, that roles and responsibilities outlined in local charters or ordinances may differ from those described here.

Administrative Responsibilities of Public Managers

Beyond the general responsibilities outlined in the statutes, managers are expected to perform a variety of administrative duties. The most important of these are discussed below.

Manage Services

A public manager is expected to oversee the administration of the services provided by the city or county. These services may include

- Public works
- Public safety
- Planning and economic development
- Parks and recreation
- Resource recovery and recycling
- Libraries
- Health and human services
- Utilities

**Table 1.   Statutory Roles and Responsibilities of
North Carolina Municipal Elected Officials and City Managers**

Mayor

1. Presides at council meetings. (G.S. 160A-69)
2. Calls special meetings of the council. (G.S. 160A-71)
3. Votes to break a tie or may vote on all matters. (G.S. 160A-69) In a city where the mayor is elected by the council from among its membership and the city charter makes no provision as to the right of the mayor to vote, he or she has the right to vote as a council member on all matters before the council but does not have the right to break a tie vote in which he or she participated. The mayor *cannot* veto actions of the board and *cannot* appoint or remove members without the board's permission.
4. Assumes all powers and duties enumerated in the General Statutes as well as any others conferred on him or her by the council. The mayor is recognized as the official head of the city for the purpose of serving civil process (G.S. 160A-67) and most federal and state agencies extend this same recognition for the purpose of official correspondence or actions, such as the approval of grants or the enforcement of federal laws and regulations.

Council

1. Authorized to organize and reorganize city government. Except when expressly prevented by other laws, the council may "…create, change, abolish, and consolidate offices, positions, departments, boards, commissions, and agencies . . . to promote orderly and efficient administration of city affairs . . . ."(G.S. 160A-146)
2. "Except as otherwise provided by law, the government and general management of the city shall be vested in the council." (G.S. 160A-67)
3. Confers powers and duties upon the mayor pursuant to law. (G.S. 160A-67).
4. In a council–manager city, the council as a body appoints the city manager to serve at its pleasure (G.S. 160A-147) and as the employer of the manager, the council is the body to which the manager is directly responsible and accountable.

City Manager

1. Directs and supervises the administration of all departments, offices, and agencies of the city, subject to the general direction and control of the council, except as otherwise provided by law. (G.S. 160A-148)
2. Appoints and suspends or removes all city officers and employees not elected by the people and whose appointment or removal is not otherwise provided for by law, except the city attorney, in accordance with the general personnel rules, regulations, policies, or ordinances adopted by the council. (G.S. 160A-148)
3. Sees that all laws of the state, the city charter, and the ordinances, resolutions, and regulations of the council are faithfully executed within the city. (G.S. 160A-148)
4. Attends all meetings of the council and recommends any measures that he or she deems expedient. (G.S. 160A-148)
5. Prepares and submits the annual budget and capital program to the council. (G.S. 160A-148)
6. Annually submits to the council and makes available to the public a complete report on the finances and administrative activities of the city as of the end of the fiscal year. (G.S. 160A-148)
7. Makes any other reports that the council may require concerning the operations of city departments, offices, and agencies subject to the city manager's direction and control. (G.S. 160A-148)
8. Performs any other duties that may be required or authorized by the council. (G.S. 160A-148)

Table 2. Statutory Roles and Responsibilities of
North Carolina County Commissioners and County Managers

Board Chair (G.S. 153A-39)

1. Serves as the presiding officer.
2. Votes on measures before the board.
3. Calls special meetings.
4. Declares state of emergency.
5. Uses authority to direct persons who disrupt a meeting to leave.
6. Assumes other duties conferred by the board of commissioners.

Commissioners (G.S. 153A-76)

1. Create, change, abolish, and consolidate county government.
2. Change the composition and manner of selection of boards, commissions, and agencies.
3. Promote orderly and efficient administration of county affairs, but may not
   - abolish what is required by law.
   - take actions specifically forbidden by law.
   - stop or reassign a function or duty assigned by law.
   - change the composition or selection of the local board of education, board of health, board of social services, board of elections, or board of alcoholic beverage control.

County Manager (G.S. 153A-82)

1. Appoints with the approval of the board of commissioners and suspends or removes all county officers, employees, and agents except those who are elected by the people or whose appointment is otherwise provided for by law.
2. Directs and supervises the administration of all county offices, departments, boards, commissions, and agencies under the general control of the board of commissioners, subject to the general direction and control of the board.
3. Attends all meetings of the board of commissioners and recommends any measures considered expedient.
4. Sees that the orders, ordinances, resolutions, and regulations of the board of commissioners are faithfully executed within the county.
5. Prepares and submits the annual budget and capital program to the board of commissioners.
6. Annually submits to the board of commissioners and makes available to the public a complete report on the finances and administrative activities of the county as of the end of the fiscal year.
7. Makes any other reports that the board of commissioners may require concerning the operations of county offices, departments, boards, commissions, and agencies.
8. Performs any other duties that may be required or authorized by the board of commissioners.

Although they are not expected to have expertise in all of these areas, managers should have some general knowledge about each service the city or county provides. Department heads typically oversee day-to-day operations and regularly report to the manager. In small communities, however, the manager may act as head of all departments and oversee their operations. An effective city or county manager understands local government services and helps department heads and employees meet current expectations and anticipate future needs.

Prepare Agenda Materials for Board/Council Meetings

City and county managers work with the board's presiding officer and other board members to prepare meeting agendas. During the agenda planning process, the manager assists others in identifying the issues to be discussed, setting the order of the agenda, and providing supportive materials to board members in advance of the meeting. A properly prepared agenda packet and a well-organized meeting structure allow board members to arrive prepared and to use their time effectively during meetings.

Develop Strategic Goals for the Organization

The manager works with elected officials to develop short- and long-term goals for local government. This strategic planning process should provide a vision for the future and specific steps for achieving that vision. A comprehensive approach to strategic planning involves envisioning the organization's goals, enacting a plan, and evaluating results, as illustrated in Figure 1, below.

Facilitate Leadership

A facilitative leader involves others in developing, implementing, and achieving the organization's goals. Effective public managers share information and ideas gathered from elected officials, employees, and citizens and encourage collaboration among various groups. Facilitative leadership promotes the sharing of information and ensures that everyone is given an opportunity to contribute to the organization's success.

Maintain Quality Workforce

A manager is expected to plan for and supervise much of the city's or county's workforce. The manager may or may not play a direct role in recruiting and hiring employees, but he or she is ultimately responsible for all employees in the organization except those who are by law appointed by the governing board or directly elected to their positions (for example, registers of deeds, sheriffs, and tax assessors). Of the employees hired by a manager, the most important are the department heads, who report directly to the manager and serve

Figure 1.   Strategic Public Leadership: Setting Priorities and Getting Results

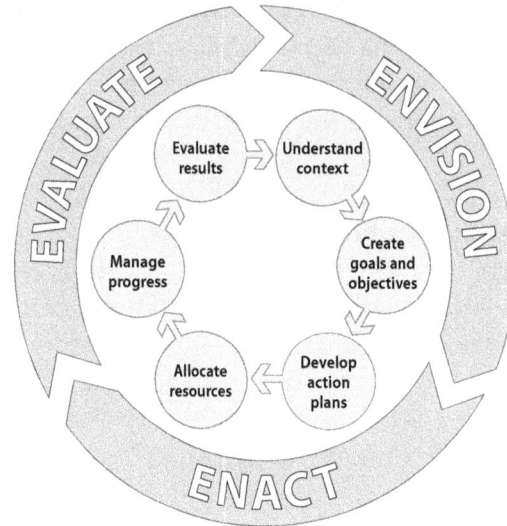

as members of the management team. A successful manager must be able to select quality employees who can be trusted to do their jobs without constant oversight. Managers also may be involved in human resource activities such as strategic workforce planning, employee training, performance reviews, and disciplinary actions.

Manage Resources

Public managers need to be knowledgeable about funding sources, resource management, and financial accountability.[4] In larger organizations, a manager works with a finance officer and/or a budget officer to oversee the organization's finances. Effective managers think strategically about the organization's mix of resources, recognizing trade-offs that accompany different funding sources and financial obligations. Local governments in North Carolina make short- and long-term capital investments, generate a mix of private and public funds, and provide a variety of public services. Managers need to ensure that resources are used and accounted for according to the law.

By law, managers in North Carolina are required to propose to the governing board a balanced budget. This budget needs to be comprehensive and must provide sufficient

---

4. For more information on funding sources, see Kara A. Millonzi, *Local Government Revenue Sources in North Carolina* (UNC School of Government, 2011).

information to allow the board or council to understand where the money will come from and how it will be allocated to provide services to citizens. It is the manager's responsibility (not the governing board's) to propose a balanced budget.

Once the manager has submitted a proposed budget to the board, it is the board's job to determine what is politically feasible and what members are willing to support. Under North Carolina law, both the manager's proposed budget and the final budget adopted by the board must be balanced. Ideally a manager will have experience in preparing budgets. An inexperienced public manager may need the assistance and support of a team of individuals with experience in preparing and presenting local government budgets.

The manager is also responsible for making sure the local government has its financial house in order. He or she must abide by state laws and local policies in managing the financial resources as they are distributed to departments for the provision of services and for employees' salaries and benefits. The budget specifies where all funds are supposed to go and how they are to be used; the manager is responsible for making sure that happens.

Preparing to Hire a Manager

The first step in a successful search is to prepare well. Members of the local governing board should come to agreement on what kind of manager the local government needs. The board also must determine what process it will use in selecting the manager. Additionally, the board may need to appoint an interim manager until a new manager can be hired.

The board's commitment to the search is vitally important to successful results. If board members disagree about what the local government needs, what hiring procedures they will use, or what qualities the new manager should possess, their discord will be readily apparent to candidates during the hiring process, and qualified candidates may withdraw from the search.

The most successful hiring process was also the simplest and most straightforward. What made this process successful was the groundwork laid by both parties prior to the interview process. When the interview actually took place . . . we were able to openly and frankly discuss the board's expectations of a manager and the challenges of the position.

Identifying the Community's Goals and Future Directions

What constitutes a good manager for an organization differs according to the needs of the community, the local government, and the governing board. For example, a person with strong financial planning experience may be needed in one community, while another community may need someone who has been successful in developing productive public–private partnerships or public works. When preparing to hire a manager, members of a governing board must first identify shared goals for the community and local government. They should also be clear and in agreement about the future they want for their community.

A review of historical documents can give elected officials a sense of what the community has done well over time and how it has handled challenges. Recent planning documents and updated progress reports can provide perspective on what the current priorities are and what still needs to be done to address pressing needs. With a clear picture of the organization's past and present, the board will be better able to articulate the community's goals and future direction. It can then narrow its focus and identify the essential skills needed in a new manager. The discussion questions below are designed to facilitate this process.

I believe the board had a good understanding of what its challenges were and what kind of experience, expertise, and personality it would take for a manager to be successful in meeting its goals and objectives. It's important for the process to be balanced—that is, for the board and the candidate to bring an equal amount to the table. Both have something to offer, and both have something they want in return.

Questions for Discussion

1. What is the history of our local government?
   - Paint a historical picture. Refer to local charters, organizational records, meeting minutes, news articles, and other documents to create a timeline of major events that have occurred in the community.
   - Take time to reflect. Where has local government been successful in advancing the community's goals? Who helped make things happen? What contributed to success? When were there difficulties for the community and/or local government? How have people responded to crises? How has local government planned for the future?

2. How long has our local government had a public manager? What has been the role of the public manager over time? How has it changed? How has it remained consistent?

3. What are our local government's strengths? What challenges does it face? Are there major projects or issues that require attention? What external forces are affecting local government (for example, political, economic, societal, or technological factors)? Does the organization have a strategic plan?

4. What are our hopes and dreams for the future of the community and how will local government play a part in making this vision a reality? What will local government need to be and do into the future?

Agreeing on a Hiring Process

Members of the board also must agree on the process that will be used in hiring a manager. There are many options to consider. The process for a board that has already identified an internal candidate will be considerably different than that of a board that wants to pursue a national search. Whether to hire an external firm or conduct the search internally is another factor to consider. Some boards prefer to use a public process, while others opt to keep candidates' names confidential. Note, however, that in North Carolina, a local governing board may not disclose any information about applicants for the position of manager to anyone other than the board members without a waiver signed by the applicant.[1] The discussion questions below are designed to help board members agree on a hiring process.

Do not leave the important work of the hiring process up to outside consultants. A board may use consultants to recruit and to narrow the list of qualified candidates to be sure the finalists meet the criteria set by the board, but the job of hiring must be carried out by the board itself.

Questions for Discussion

1. What process are we going to use to hire a manager?
2. Will the search be internal or external? Local or national?
3. Should we hire an executive search firm?
4. Where will we advertise to attract a pool of qualified candidates?
5. Who will review applications and interview candidates?
6. How will candidates' experience and interpersonal skills be assessed?
7. What process will be used for narrowing the applicant pool and making a final selection?
8. What is an appropriate salary range?
9. How will we involve employees and the public in the hiring process?

---

1. *See* Sections 160A-168 (cities) and 153A-98 (counties) of the North Carolina General Statutes (hereinafter G.S.); Elkin Tribune v. Yadkin Cnty. Bd. of Cnty. Comm'rs, 331 N.C. 735 (1992).

Hiring an Interim Manager

While the governing board is making decisions about how to go about hiring a new manager, the organization still needs to have someone in place to provide day-to-day oversight and management. Local governments often appoint an interim manager to assume responsibility for these duties. North Carolina local governments that operate under the board–manager form of government are statutorily required to appoint an interim manager.[2]

Municipal boards may not appoint a member of the council to serve as interim manager—the mayor and council members are required to assign the interim role to someone else.[3] North Carolina law permits boards of county commissioners to assign the role of interim manager to a member of the board. This could be the board chair or another member with appropriate skills who is willing to assume this responsibility.

Under the council–manager form of government in North Carolina, if an interim manager is not appointed, no employees can be hired or fired, because the governing board does not have the authority to hire or fire employees other than the manager or interim manager.[4] Nor can the board of a municipality whose charter provides for the council–manager form of government automatically revert to operating under the mayor–council form of government until a full-time manager is hired. Municipal governments must therefore be prepared to appoint an interim manager if necessary.

Interim managers come from a variety of places. The interim manager may be appointed from within the organization—often, he or she is an assistant or deputy manager or department head who is willing to serve in this capacity until a permanent manager can be hired. A person who is currently looking for a permanent manager's job may be a good candidate for an interim position. Retired managers are sometimes willing to provide short-term assistance. Management services also are available through private firms. The North Carolina League of Municipalities and the North Carolina Association of County Commissioners maintain lists of potential interim managers. The North Carolina Regional Councils of Governments are also a good resource for finding people who can provide interim support during the search process.

Governing boards sometimes appoint someone they are considering hiring as a full-time manager to fill the interim position. Appointing an internal candidate or a manager in transition as interim manager enables board members to see how the person conducts himself or herself in the position before making a final decision. If the governing board intends to hire the person it appoints to the interim management position, going through

---

2. G.S. 160A-150.
3. G.S. 160A-151.
4 .G.S. 160A-148(1).

an elaborate search process is usually unnecessary. Except in rare instances in which a governing board wants to compare the internal candidate to well-qualified external candidates, the search process can be streamlined and the board can offer the interim manager the full-time position, conduct background checks, and begin negotiating the terms of employment.

Do not pursue an elaborate selection process if the board has its mind made up to appoint an internal candidate. When there is an internal candidate and others know it, individuals are usually reluctant to participate because they do not want to go through a fake process.

An interim manager is responsible for keeping the organization operating smoothly, troubleshooting day-to-day issues, keeping the governing board informed, and supporting the board's work. He or she can also help establish procedures for turning things over to a new manager. The discussion questions below are designed to help a board make decisions about hiring an interim manager.

Questions for Discussion
1. What do we want to do about interim management? What kind of support does the local government need?
2. How will we select the interim manager?
3. Are we considering hiring someone within the organization as the permanent manager? If so, do we want to give this individual an opportunity to demonstrate his or her readiness for the role by serving as the interim manager?
4. Are we interested in appointing an external candidate, such as a manager in transition, as interim manager?
5. What are the pros and cons of using an external interim manager?
6. What are we prepared to pay an external interim manager and for how long?

Getting the Right Fit

One of the most important keys to a public manager's success is being a good fit with the local governing board, the local government, and the community. While knowledge, skills, and abilities are important, they are not the only factors that contribute to a manager's success. Even seasoned managers may find it difficult to adapt to new settings: for example, someone who has worked in an urban environment may not be comfortable in a rural setting, or a person who has been successful as a city manager may find it difficult to shift to county management. Successful hires are those that are a good fit for both the organization and the applicant. The discussion questions on page 20 are designed to help board members identify the best type of manager for their community's unique situation.

Some managers are better suited for small towns and others are suited for larger communities. The key is to find the right match. The council, town citizens, and manager all need to be relatively happy with each other.

Competencies

The International City/County Management Association (ICMA) lists the following core competencies as essential to effective management:[1]

- Policy facilitation
- Citizen participation
- Citizen service
- Democratic advocacy
- Vision

---

1. "Practices for Effective Local Government," International City/County Management Association, accessed July 25, 2011, http://icma.org/en/university/about/management_practices/overview.

- Quality assurance
- Functional and operational expertise and planning
- Strategic planning
- Technological literacy
- Diversity
- Human resource management
- Financial analysis
- Budgeting
- Staff effectiveness
- Media relations
- Presentation skills
- Initiative
- Integrity
- Creativity and innovation
- Personal development
- Advocacy and interpersonal communication

Every candidate will have strengths and weaknesses in these areas, and it is up to the governing board to decide which characteristics are most important to the organization. Board members may want to start with a comprehensive list of competencies and then narrow the list to five or so characteristics that they consider most important in a manager. The board can then develop a profile of its ideal candidate, and every finalist for the position should match that profile. Many individuals may be qualified for the job, but only a few will be a good fit for the organization. The exercise in Appendix 2, Practices for Effective Local Government Management, is designed to help governing boards identify the management practices that are most important to their organization.

The board should understand what type of person it needs based upon knowledge of the organizational structure, strengths, and weaknesses. Hiring a great professional with the wrong background for the organization can be a fatal mistake.

Credentials

If board members believe that it's important to hire a credentialed manager, they may want to seek candidates who are members of the International City/County Management Association (ICMA). The ICMA has more than 18,000 members who fit the criteria for professional membership. Nearly one thousand managers have completed the ICMA's Voluntary Credentialing Program, which entails more than forty hours of advanced professional development. Members of the ICMA are committed to the association's code of ethics. They may also participate in the ICMA's Knowledge Network, which allows members to interact with one another to share advice and information with fellow managers.[2]

The North Carolina City and County Management Association (NCCCMA) is the professional association for city and county managers and assistant managers from counties and municipalities in North Carolina. Its members subscribe to a high standard of professionalism, including conformance with the ICMA Code of Ethics.[3]

Job Description

Once the board has agreed on a profile of the idea candidate, it can come up with a detailed outline of what it expects from an incoming manager. Typically, a number of people are involved in creating this detailed job description. Stakeholders in this process may include the following:

- *Board/Council.* What kind of communication do they expect to have with the manager? What characteristics are important to working well with the board? Are there projects the board is particularly interested in pursuing that would require expertise in a specific field?
- *Organization.* What type of oversight do department heads expect from the manager? Does the organization need someone with in-depth knowledge of a particular area or someone able to facilitate work across departments? What qualities or background do department heads, supervisors, and employees prefer in a manager? What personal characteristics are important?
- *Citizens.* What kind of work background and expertise do community stakeholders want in a county or city manager? What do they expect from local government leaders? What do they consider priorities for local government?[4]

---

2. For more information, see the ICMA website, http://icma.org.

3. For more information, see the NCCCMA website, www.ncmanagers.org.

4. For more information on how to involve the community, see John B. Stephens, Ricardo S. Morse, and Kelley T. O'Brien, *Public Outreach and Participation* (UNC School of Government, 2011).

The job description should clearly state what the manager is expected to accomplish in the job. The board may also want to agree on a set of priorities that the manager will be expected to address during the first year.

Identify key expectations of the next manager and prioritize them. Every finalist should have qualifications that are on the priority list.

Questions for Discussion

1. What competencies are most important for the new manager to be successful?
2. Do we want a manager with credentials from a professional management association, such as ICMA or NCCCMA?
3. What responsibilities will the new manager have?
4. What projects are currently underway that the manager would have to oversee?
5. What projects are currently being discussed or debated?
6. What mutual obligations/expectations should the board and manager have to help ensure success?
7. What support and assistance will be offered when and by whom? Will a mentor or coach be hired?[5]
8. What will the short-term goals be for the first three months? For the first six months? For the first year?
9. How will the manager get feedback during the first year?[6]

---

5. A mentor can be beneficial when the incoming manager is not familiar with the area. Familiarizing the manager with local knowledge and cultural awareness can introduce the manager to the community and ease his or her transition.

6. A review of written goals and board expectations every three or four months during the first year can improve communication and understanding between both parties.

Finding a Manager

The process of finding a new manager is usually a lengthy one. A four- to six-month period of recruiting is common, but it is important to take as much time as necessary to get the right person. Table 3 presents a timetable for the search.

Table 3.   Reasonable Recruiting Timetable for a City or County Manager

STEP	AMOUNT OF TIME	
	TYPICAL	FAST
Determine needs	1 Week	1 Week
Draft and post job ad	2 Weeks	1 Week
Recruit applicants	8 Weeks	6 Weeks
Screen applicants	3 Weeks	1 Week
Assess candidates	6 Weeks	4 Weeks
Hire manager	1 Week	1 Week
LENGTH OF SEARCH:	19 Weeks/5 Months	13 Weeks/3 Months
Manager makes decision and reports	2 Months	1 Month
TOTAL LENGTH OF PROCESS:	7 Months	4 Months

Source: Adapted from Kurt Jenne, "Hiring a City or County Manager," *Popular Government* 62, no. 3 (Spring 1997): 33.

Figure 2 on page 22 presents an overview of the hiring process. The necessary stages and steps are discussed below.

Figure 2. Hiring Flow Chart

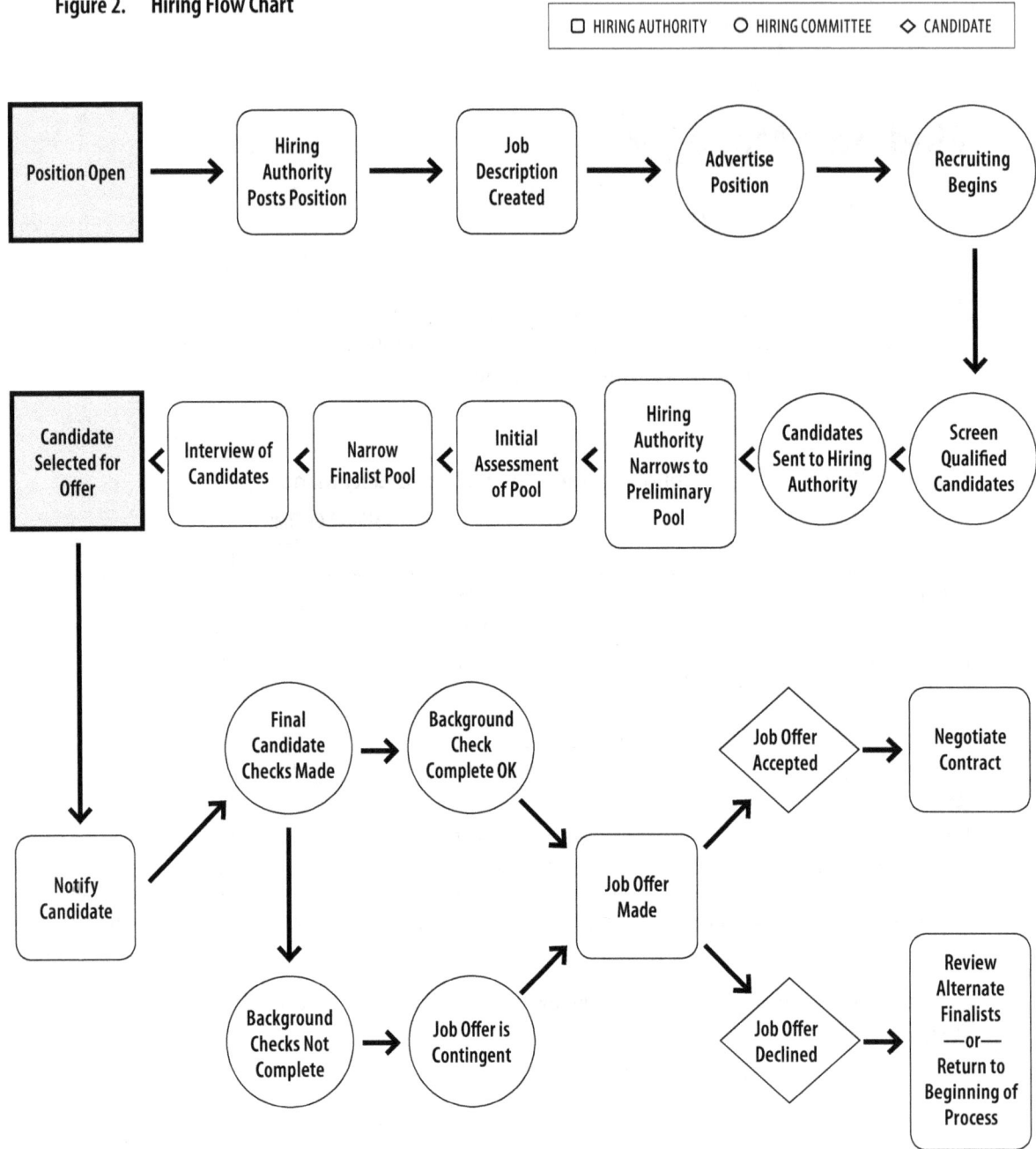

☐ HIRING AUTHORITY   ◯ HIRING COMMITTEE   ◇ CANDIDATE

Position Open → Hiring Authority Posts Position → Job Description Created → Advertise Position → Recruiting Begins

Candidate Selected for Offer ← Interview of Candidates ← Narrow Finalist Pool ← Initial Assessment of Pool ← Hiring Authority Narrows to Preliminary Pool ← Candidates Sent to Hiring Authority ← Screen Qualified Candidates

Notify Candidate → Final Candidate Checks Made

Final Candidate Checks Made → Background Check Complete OK → Job Offer Made

Final Candidate Checks Made → Background Checks Not Complete → Job Offer is Contingent → Job Offer Made

Job Offer Made → Job Offer Accepted → Negotiate Contract

Job Offer Made → Job Offer Declined → Review Alternate Finalists —or— Return to Beginning of Process

Source: Adapted from Catherine D. Fyock, *Hiring Source Book* (Society for Human Resources Management, 2003).

Advertising the Position

The job advertisement should reflect the local government's direction and goals and the characteristics the board wants in a manager. The board may prefer a candidate from the state or region, or it may be open to looking at national candidates. If the board wants someone who is familiar with the area, people, and customs, its search strategy needs to be designed to attract people who possess this knowledge. If the board is looking for someone unfamiliar with the residents and politics of the community who can come in without bias and bring fresh ideas to the community, the search strategy needs to be designed to attract people from outside the region.

Job openings are typically listed on the local government's website and in local and regional media. The websites and publications of professional organizations—such as the North Carolina League of Municipalities, the North Carolina Association of County Commissioners, the International City/County Management Association, and the North Carolina City and County Management Association are also good ways to reach qualified candidates.

Conducting the Search

One of the first things a board needs to decide is whether it will contract with a search firm or an external contractor or whether the search will be handled locally by the board and other internal personnel. These options are discussed in detail below. No matter which option the board chooses, the criteria and standards used to screen applicants should be determined in advance and should relate directly to the priorities set forth in the job description.

The board should first decide if it could be beneficial to hire a consultant to assist in the process. If elected officials are routinely involved in senior staff hiring and firing decisions, the board may be qualified to handle the process internally with some clerical and administrative assistance. If the board lacks that experience, external professional assistance is beneficial.

Using a Search Firm or Other External Contractor

Using an executive search firm is an option for cities or counties that can afford it. The cost of a search firm's services typically ranges from 30 percent to 33 percent of a candidate's expected annual compensation.[1]

---

1. Walter U. Baker, "The Hunt for Top Talent: 11 Questions to Ask Prospective Search Firms," The Riley Guide, accessed August 3, 2011, www.rileyguide.com/articles/wubaker.html.

A search firm will typically provide some or all of the following services:

- Develop a recruitment strategy in conjunction with the board
- Develop a job description/profile in conjunction with the board
- Establish criteria for candidates in conjunction with the board
- Set a timeline for the recruitment, interview, and hiring process
- Create a recruitment campaign—including advertising the job opening via newspapers, magazines, professional publications, job websites, and other media
- Contact potential candidates
- Screen candidates by reviewing resumes, checking references, and assessing skills
- Complete background checks on chosen finalists
- Submit recommendations to the board
- Keep the process focused on finding a manager rather than resolving internal issues in the board or organization

An external firm may also help the board by providing guidance on how to

- Interview finalists
- Negotiate contract, salary, and benefits
- Notify rejected candidates

Hiring a search firm may result in a higher number of qualified candidates. A search firm with experience can also make the formal hiring process easier—particularly if members of the board lack experience in hiring. Additionally, a search firm can act as a neutral facilitator to help a board reach consensus.

If the board decides to hire a search firm, it should carefully evaluate and interview at least two firms before making a selection. A well-qualified firm will have experience in finding and recruiting talented candidates for similar positions. Because the representative who serves as the initial contact with the board may not be the person who will conduct the actual search, it is important to ask who will be doing the work and who is ultimately accountable for the search process. The lead consultant should have a clear understanding of the type of candidate the board is seeking and the ways in which the board will evaluate candidates. The firm should be able to provide a reliable estimate of how long the search will take, and the timeline and deliverables should be part of its contract with the board.

The board should also ask for an agreement that the search firm will not recruit from its organization for a specified length of time after the manager has been hired.[2]

Not every firm is right for every search. The following worksheet is designed to help a board identify a qualified search firm.

WORKSHEET: *Questions to Ask When Choosing a Search Firm*

Is the firm accredited?

_____

_____

How much experience does the firm have with local government manager searches?

_____

_____

How are the fees and expenses structured?

_____

_____

Who will be the lead consultant responsible for the search process?

_____

_____

What is the timeline for the search?

_____

_____

What is the firm's success rate?

_____

_____

_____

_____

2. Walter U. Baker, "The Hunt for Top Talent: 11 Questions to Ask Prospective Search Firms," The Riley Guide, accessed August 3, 2011, www.rileyguide.com/articles/wubaker.html.

Does the firm have a policy that prevents it from recruiting in an area where it has recently placed an employee?

_____

_____

_____

How are reference checks handled?

_____

_____

What is the firm's role in negotiating an employment agreement?

_____

_____

_____

Conducting a Local Search

A local search is appropriate if a board has identified candidates who already work for the local government and are interested in being promoted to the manager's position. A city or county, a regional Council of Government, or even a nearby university may conduct a local search, focusing on candidates within the community, region, or state. Assistance with the search process is available from the North Carolina City and County Management Association, the North Carolina League of Municipalities, and the North Carolina Association of County Commissioners.

Even if a search will be handled locally, the vetting and assessment process remains critical to making an effective hire. A local search is usually less expensive than one conducted by an external firm, but it takes considerably more time and effort on the part of elected officials and other local government employees, such as the interim manager, the human resources director, and various department heads.

The Board's Responsibility

Regardless of whether a search is done by a firm or by the local government itself, members of the board are ultimately responsible for the hiring decision. The board must work diligently to hire a manager who will serve the board, the organization, and the community well.

The board also has a responsibility to the candidates. Board members need to recognize that the process is stressful for the candidates, and they should be mindful of their concerns. The board should clearly communicate where it is in the process and how long each step will take. Having the clerk or a trusted designee contact candidates to keep them informed is a good way of letting them know that they are valued and that their time and effort are appreciated.

The following worksheet is designed to help the board plan the hiring process.

WORKSHEET: *Job Search Planning*

PLANNING THE PROCESS

What are short and long-term priorities for local government?

_____
_____
_____

What is the profile of the ideal candidate?

_____
_____
_____

What do governing board members expect from the search process?

_____
_____
_____

Will the governing board use an external search firm or consultant or will it conduct the search internally?

_____
_____
_____

What is the time frame for the search?

_____
_____
_____

What evaluation criteria will be used to assess candidate qualifications?

_____
_____
_____

Who will write the job description and advertisement?

_____
_____
_____

Who will be responsible for advertising the position?

_____
_____
_____

Who will screen the applications?

_____
_____
_____

Who will structure the interview process?

_____
_____
_____

Who will set up the interviews?

_____
_____
_____

Who will do reference and background checks?

_____
_____
_____

Who will negotiate the contract? Who will communicate with the candidates not selected?

_____
_____
_____

CONDUCTING THE SEARCH

At what level will the search be conducted (internal, local, statewide, national)?

_____
_____
_____

How many candidates will the board interview?

_____
_____
_____

How will the interviews be conducted?

_____

_____

_____

Who will participate in the interviews?

_____

_____

_____

What system will be used to assess candidate qualifications?

_____

_____

_____

CLOSING THE SEARCH

Who will be responsible for offering the position to the selected candidate?

_____

_____

_____

Who will notify individuals who were not selected?

_____

_____

_____

What will be the terms of employment (direct compensation, benefits, allowances, etc.)?

_____

_____

_____

Will there be a probationary period? If so, what are the terms?

_____

_____

_____

What are three to five priorities for the new manager?

_____

_____

_____

What are the board's expectations of the manager during the first three months? The first six months? The first year?

_____

_____

_____

The Board's Role

Whether it conducts a local search or hires a search firm, the board needs to be involved in three important parts of the hiring process: screening applicants, assessing candidates, and making a job offer. During the screening process, the board should decide which applicants to invite for interviews. The board should then take an active role in interviewing candidates for the position. Finally, the board must reach consensus on which candidate to hire and make an offer.

Do not go through the process until the board is one on what the process will be and how a final candidate will be selected. You do not want to make it up as you go through the steps.

Screening Applicants

As part of the planning process, the board needs to determine how applicants will be screened. Typically, the work of determining which applicants meet the board's criteria is delegated to a subcommittee of the board (or to a search firm).[1] It is inadvisable to have a single person, such as the board chair or the mayor, responsible for screening applicants. In situations where members of the board do not trust each other to screen applicants fairly, the screening process can be completed by the full board, so long as the total number of applications is manageable. If, however, there are hundreds of applications, the time it would take for the full board to review every application becomes burdensome. In such a situation, the board would probably need to resort to a search firm.

---

1. If two or more board members are appointed to a committee, the committee is considered a public body and is subject to the open meetings laws. See David M. Lawrence, *Open Meetings and Local Governments in North Carolina* (UNC School of Government, 7th edition 2008).

It is important to identify a screening process that can be applied consistently for all applicants. Screening may be done in any of the following ways:[2]

1. The board may select a trusted staff member (or hire a search firm) to receive applications and sort them according to whether or not the applicant appears to meet the minimum requirements designated by the board. The applications of those who are deemed to meet the basic requirements may then be submitted to a subcommittee of the board (if there is a designated search committee) or to the entire board for review and consideration.

2. The board may designate a subcommittee of board members to receive applications, sort them into the categories (as above), and conduct an initial screening for the whole board. No single individual should be given full responsibility for this task. The subcommittee can narrow the pool and submit a shortened list of candidates to the full board. The list should contain twice as many candidates as the board plans to interview.

3. The entire board can review every applicant and compile the short list together. If the full board is reviewing all of the applications, it typically does so with the help of a third party, such as the board's clerk or attorney or the director of human resources.

The board's decision about whom to interview may be more difficult if there are a number of well-qualified candidates. The board should decide in advance how it will further narrow the pool if necessary. Board members may want to develop a detailed questionnaire to further screen applicants before inviting them to formal interviews. After the board has made its selections, candidates who did not qualify for the position should be thanked for their interest and informed that they are no longer being considered for the position.

At the end of the screening process, the board should create a final list of candidates—typically three to seven—who will be invited to come in for formal interviews. It is important for the board to select finalists that it believes will be a good fit. Interviewing is a time-consuming process for the candidates and for those conducting the interviews, so the board should interview only those people it genuinely thinks it would like to employ. At this point the board may also want to conduct full background checks (discussed in more detail below) on the finalists for the position.

---

2. Kurt Jenne, "Hiring a City or County Manager," *Popular Government* 62, no. 3 (Spring 1997): 26-33.

Assessing Candidates

Boards and other stakeholders may assess candidates in a number of ways. The most commonly used methods are discussed below.

Conducting the Interviews

Interviews are the most common technique used to assess a candidate's character, skill, and fit for the job. Prior to bringing people in for interviews, board members and management team members participating in the interview process should compile a standard set of questions that will be asked of all the final candidates. Often, each member of the board is given an opportunity to interview each final candidate one-on-one before the board as a whole conducts a group interview. Standard interview questions should be used for each individual interview as well as for the group interviews. Asking every candidate the same questions in the same order results in a fairer interview process for the candidates and makes it easier for board members to compare them.

Communicate your vision of the community and the manager's role in achieving that vision early in the process. Strive for honesty and integrity during the interview and provide opportunities for the candidate to ask the board members questions about the board, the local government, and the community.

Board members should also be aware that impressions can affect an interview. Most people form impressions within the first few seconds of meeting someone and quickly jump to a conclusion about the person's character based on a few initial observations. If a candidate makes a strong first impression, an interviewer may pose easy questions so that the candidate performs well, reinforcing the interviewer's first impression. Similarly, a poor initial impression may lead the interviewer to challenge the candidate in order to reinforce the interviewer's impression. A technique that can help interviewers balance this instinctual response is to have them quickly write down their first impression, ask all candidates the same questions, and then compare their initial impression with their assessment of each candidate at the end of the interview.

The following sample questions might be asked in the interview:

- Why do you want this job?
- What can you bring to this job that others can't?
- Why did you leave/do you want to leave your previous/current job?
- What do you consider your strengths in management?
- What do you consider your weaknesses?

- What do you see as areas of opportunity for this city or county?
- How would you take advantage of these opportunities?
- What three words describe you?
- How do you define success?
- How have you handled a major leadership challenge in the past?
- What is a mistake that you've made and what did you learn from it?
- What is your approach to dealing with staff members who are reluctant to speak up?
- What are some of the ways in which you motivate your staff?
- How do you network with peers in this field?
- How would you describe your management/leadership style in working with boards of elected officials?
- If you were hired, would you consider this a long-term position (more than five years) or a short-term stepping stone to a higher position?

Some questions are illegal to ask: for example, questions about the person's political or religious views or whether he or she plans to have children. Asking such questions is discriminatory and could result in charges being filed with the U.S. Equal Employment Opportunity Commission. In general, it is best to avoid asking any questions related to personal views that do not affect job performance. Appendix 3 provides a list of questions that may and may not be asked of an interviewee.

Some topics are delicate or controversial, but the board should never hold back information from the candidates about current or future problems or concerns. If a manager is hired and finds out after the fact that members of the board were not forthcoming about issues confronting the town or county, the individual will likely have a difficult time trusting other information shared by the board. If the town or county is facing major challenges, it is better to hire someone who is already aware of the problems and ready to tackle them.

> *Board members and candidates need to be honest and forthright with each other. If the board wants to continue organizational practices and make changes slowly, the candidate needs to know that. If the board is expecting a significant shift in direction and staffing changes are thought to be needed, the candidate needs to know that. Not everyone is suited for or up to both of those opposite approaches.*

The board should also make sure there is time during the interview process for the candidate to ask questions of the board members. A candidate might want to ask board members the following questions:

- Why did you get involved in local government?
- How long have you been in your role?
- What are your goals, and how can I help you reach them?
- What, in your view, is the ideal manager?

Candidates should be proactive and spend time doing some background work in order to uncover any information that could possibly deter them from taking the position if it is offered. Candidates should also be aware of board dynamics during the group interview, because board members who do not get along with each other can make the manager's job much more difficult.

> *I believe my worst experience with a hiring/selection process came from an opportunity that seemed like a perfect match based on my age and experience. I was enthusiastic when I arrived for the interview but quickly realized that the board was extremely partisan and much more concerned with their political agenda than with the qualifications of a competent manager. . . . Had I done my homework ahead of time, I would not have even considered sitting for an interview.*

The setting for the interview is also important. If the local government facility is crowded and noisy, it is advisable to hold interviews off-site in a place where people can meet without being interrupted. One-on-one interviews can be held in small offices or conference rooms. For group interviews, a U-shaped setup with the candidate at a separate table in the middle allows members of the board to see each other as well as the candidate during the interview. There should also be sufficient time between candidate interviews for board members to make notes about what they heard and their impressions of the person being interviewed. If interviews with multiple people are scheduled back-to-back, it may be difficult for board members to recall which person said what.

During the face-to-face interview process, candidates typically take a tour of the town and have a chance to meet with department heads and other local officials. They may even check out schools and available homes. Sometimes a spouse or partner is invited to do this as well.

For the process to be successful, it is important that the manager and his or her family enter the job with eyes wide open and that they are happy in the community.

As the board narrows the pool of candidates, it may decide to invite two to three finalists for a second interview. Especially in smaller communities, it may be preferable to hold the second-round interviews in a more relaxed social setting and invite spouses or partners to attend. If the candidate is going to take the job, it is critical for the person and his or her family to feel welcome and comfortable in the community. Just as the board is looking at the candidate to determine if the person is a good fit for the organization and community, the candidate is looking at the board, organization, and community to decide if the environment is a good fit for his or her family. The interview process works best when both the board and the candidates understand that it is a two-way conversation and both parties need to be comfortable with the outcome.

One of the best experiences I had was a public process. The board used a consultant to assist in the process. The final interviews were conducted in a public forum and on local cable television. The process was well managed and maintained a sense of professionalism.

Some boards opt to hold a public candidate forum for the final candidates. They may be asked to make public presentations in front of a live audience or to participate in a question-and-answer session broadcast by local media. Public forums give citizens and other interested groups an opportunity to learn more about the person who might become the next city or county manager. The candidates may also benefit from being able to assess how their qualifications compare to those of the other contenders. Not all candidates will agree to participate in a public process, however—particularly if they are still working for another organization or are applying for other positions. If the town or county wants the process to be public, candidates should be told what portion of the process will be open to the public and given the option to drop out of the running.

In an open process, board members are usually more guarded with their questions and responses. When the public actively participates, the interview process becomes more staged and less focused on important factors that the board and the applicant need to know about each other.

Finally, the board must decide when and how it will reveal the names of the candidates. In an open or public process, the names of candidates for the position are disclosed to local media. If the board opts to conduct an open search process, it should reveal candidates' identities only after it has narrowed its list to the few people it is seriously interested in hiring and has gotten a waiver from the finalists to have their names made public.[3]

The following worksheet is designed to help governing boards plan the interview process.

WORKSHEET: *Planning the Interview*

What does the ideal candidate profile look like for our organization?

_____

_____

_____

What are the criteria candidates must meet before they are called in for interviews?

_____

_____

_____

What are the standard questions we want to ask all candidates?

_____

_____

_____

What information will be provided to candidates prior to the interview? Will we provide a standard packet of information or will we recommend that candidates visit the organization's website and encourage them to find information on their own?

_____

_____

_____

Will we have a closed process, an open process, or some combination of both?

_____

_____

_____

Who will participate in the interviews? Will only the board members conduct interviews or will staff be involved?

_____

_____

_____

---

3. Keep in mind that North Carolina law prohibits the release of any information about the candidates to anyone other than members of the governing board without a waiver. *See* Sections 160A-168 (cities) and 153A-98 (counties) of the North Carolina General Statutes; Elkin Tribune v. Yadkin Cnty. Bd. of Cnty. Comm'rs, 331 N.C. 735 (1992).

What will be the format of the interviews? Will we interview candidates in small group settings or one at a time?

_____

_____

_____

In addition to a standard set of interview questions, will we include an assessment center where candidates' specific skills can be ranked?

_____

_____

_____

What are the trade-offs we are prepared to make when selecting finalists? Are we prepared to pay for experience or are we comfortable hiring someone who has less experience but shows promise?

_____

_____

_____

How will we communicate with members of the board and the candidates about the steps, schedule, and deadlines for the interview process?

_____

_____

_____

How will we make sure the process is fair and equitable for all candidates?

_____

_____

_____

Who will provide a welcome and take the spouse or partner on a tour of the area?

_____

_____

_____

Conducting Background Checks

Public managers have high visibility jobs and routinely interact with the public. A great deal of trust is placed in them by the governing board and the community. North Carolina governing boards are not legally required to conduct background checks on candidates, but it is highly advisable that they do so. The board should look at the employment history, financial background, and criminal records of all finalists to ensure that there are no surprises once the manager is hired.[4]

Typically, a candidate background check includes verifying all residence addresses the candidate has provided and all names he or she has used. The candidate's employment history and educational credentials[5]—including the name of the school, city and state, hours earned, degrees awarded, and honors conferred— should be verified. The background check should also cover the candidate's financial history and any criminal convictions (misdemeanor or felony).

Background checking is complicated by potential legal ramifications. Boards need as much information as possible about potential managers, including detailed checks of references, but they must be cautious in how the background check is conducted. The specific requirements for a legal background check are beyond the scope of this guide. Any governing board that decides to do background investigations on job candidates should consult a professional with experience in this area.

Once background information has been collected for the finalists, that information should be shared with board members. Any questions about an individual's background should be discussed among members of the board. If there are areas of concern, the board should decide how questions will be raised with the candidate during the interview process.

Personality Assessments

Some search firms may recommend using one or more personality assessment tools as a way to screen candidates.[6] However, personality assessments, such as the Myers-Briggs Type Indicator or Emotional Intelligence tools, are inappropriate for screening job applicants. A person's self-identification of a particular personal style or preference may not be accurate. Experienced managers, for instance, may rate themselves lower in certain areas because they are reluctant to brag about their skills. Other individuals may have inflated views of their abilities. A person who appears to be smart, well-adjusted, or competent on paper may or may not actually be that way in practice.

---

4. For a cautionary tale of what happened to one North Carolina town when it failed to look into the manager's background, see www.brunswickbeacon.com/content/town-got-snookered-commissioner-says.

5. The U.S. Department of Education's Council for Higher Education Accreditation can provide assistance in verifying whether an institution of higher education is accredited. In addition, when a candidate says that his or her degree is from an institution that is out of business, the claim can be verified with the Department of Education of the state in which the school supposedly operated.

6. If assessments are recommended by a search firm and the board agrees to their use, each candidate should be fully informed of the purpose and nature of the assessment and given a copy of the results, even if he or she is not hired.

Assessment Centers

Interviews can only tell a board so much. In addition to conducting interviews, many towns and counties have started using assessment centers to determine if a candidate would be suitable for the job. These centers are designed to assess how candidates respond in a variety of situations. This approach is helpful in assessing and comparing the strengths and weaknesses of potential candidates, but the centers are costly, difficult to set up, hard to implement, and time-consuming. Most towns and counties using assessment centers enlist the aid of a search firm with experience in setting up and conducting assessment centers for public managers.

If a board is interested in using an assessment center, it should carefully consider the following questions:

1. Who will conduct the assessment? A group of experienced assessors is needed to monitor candidates during the exercises, and each assessor needs to use a standardized method of ranking the candidates.

2. What exercises will be used? Candidates should be asked to perform tasks based on realistic, job-related scenarios, as in the following exercises:

   - *In-basket test.* In this test an applicant is given job-related memos, email messages, phone messages, and other documents. The applicant has a specified amount of time in which to prioritize the work and respond to each request or issue. This test is designed to gauge how the candidate handles the variety of demands a manager faces.

   - *Interaction exercise.* This scenario involves mock scenarios in which the candidate must interact with peers, subordinates, and residents. It is designed to reveal how the candidate treats different groups of individuals with whom a manager interacts on a regular basis.

   - *Group discussions.* In this activity, a group of candidates is seated at a round table, usually without an assigned leader. In some cases, members of the group are assigned various roles. A discussion topic or a problem is presented, and the group discusses the matter. The purpose of the activity is to discern how the candidates function in a group setting.

   - *Problem solving.* A candidate undergoing this assessment is given a problem that must be solved in a specified amount of time. Assessors observe how the candidate approaches the problem, his or her demeanor during the exercise, how he or she handles stress, and the person's overall effectiveness at solving the problem.

Assessment centers are often touted as the best way to determine a manager's strengths and weaknesses, but they are just one tool to use when searching for a manager.

Reaching Consensus and Making an Offer

The board should always keep in mind that it is more important to avoid a bad hire than to try to get the perfect fit. If the board hires a qualified candidate, in all likelihood that person will have enough positive attributes to perform the job and be successful, even if he or she does not have every single characteristic the board identified in its planning process. A bad hire, on the other hand, is difficult to overcome. If the new manager is not qualified for the position, the board, the organization, and the entire community will be adversely affected. It is also likely that the person will not stay in the job for long, and the board will find itself conducting another search soon.

> *In the end, I believe that beyond the professional, educational, and background attributes that each candidate may possess, personality, versatility, resiliency, and integrity may have more to do with ultimate success than any other factors.*

Selecting the person the board wants to hire usually requires compromise. In almost every hiring process, trade-offs will have to be made between a person's qualifications, experience, and expected salary. In some instances, the board may be comfortable hiring a less-experienced but promising person who will take the position for lower pay. In other cases, hiring someone with strong qualifications and extensive experience may be more important to the board than finding someone who will work for a lower salary. Occasionally, a board may be fortunate enough to find a candidate who is well-qualified, experienced, *and* inexpensive—for example, a retired executive receiving pension payments may agree to work as a public manager for a lower salary than someone who has not yet retired. In such instances, however, the trade-off is usually that the person will stay in the job for a shorter length of time.

No matter which candidate the board decides it would most like to hire, it should always agree on a second choice. It is very possible that the top candidate may choose not to accept the job, for any number of reasons. If that happens, the second-choice candidate should not feel slighted, nor should the board be disappointed. Board members and the selected candidate should be confident of their ability to work together.

Getting Off on the Right Foot

Once a board has selected a final candidate, it needs to agree on its expectations for the new manager. It will also need to decide what salary and benefits it is willing to offer. The manager's employment agreement should clearly spell out essential roles and responsibilities and compensation and benefits. It should also address what will happen in the event the employee is let go before the agreement expires. Additionally, the board needs to decide when and how it will evaluate the manager's performance.

> *Determine the board's goals and objectives not only for the short term but for the long term as well. Take an honest assessment of the strengths and weaknesses of the board and have a vision for the community and an idea of what you would like the manager to accomplish.*

Setting Expectations

Having a set of clear and achievable expectations, as well as clear statements about how the manager's accomplishments will be monitored, measured, and evaluated is vital to the new manager's success and helps support a strong relationship between the board and the manager. The incoming manager should be provided with a work plan that includes several priorities agreed upon by the board. If there are specific projects to be worked on or deadlines to meet, the manager must be aware of them. Any major issues the board wants addressed should be communicated to the manager early on, and the board should be careful not to add a number of additional expectations to the list too quickly. A new manager can quickly become overwhelmed and frustrated if besieged by too many requests in a short time. Individual board members should also refrain from communicating their own expectations if they are not on the list agreed upon by the entire board.

Salary and Benefits

Before extending a job offer, the board needs to have some idea of the amount it is willing and able to pay a manager. The manager's position is vital, and the individual in that position should be compensated fairly. It may be difficult for some smaller communities to keep a good manager if they cannot pay a competitive salary,[1] and such communities may be at risk of becoming training grounds for managers on the move. When determining salary level, the board should always take into account the cost of losing a good manager and the expense involved in searching for a replacement.

Benefits should also be a part of the manager's compensation, and once again, these should be fair. It is up to the board to decide what benefits to offer based on the size of the town or county, the work culture, and the types of agreements negotiated with past managers.

According to the International City/County Management Association (ICMA), benefits typically offered to managers include the following:[2]

- Health, disability, and life insurance benefits
- Vacation, sick, and military leave
- Use of a car for official business
- Retirement fund contributions
- Expense accounts
- Participation in professional activities
- Moving and relocation expenses
- Home sale and purchase expenses

Employment Agreements

Most managers have employment agreements with the municipalities or counties for which they work. Employment agreements provide safeguards for both parties. They help ensure that both the manager and the board meet their obligations. The specific expectations

---

1. The average national salary for chief executives in local government in 2010 was $106,620. U.S. Department of Labor, Bureau of Labor Statistics, Occupational Employment Statistics, www.bls.gov/oes/current/oes111011.htm.

2. "Model Employment Agreement," International City/County Management Association, accessed August 3, 2011, http://icma.org/en/icma/career_network/career_resources/model_employment_agreement.

outlined in the manager's employment agreement may also make it easier for both the manager and the board in the event of a conflict or disagreement.

Because a manager serves at the pleasure of the board, his or her employment agreement cannot specify the length of time the manager will serve (although the ICMA sets a minimum expectation of two years' service). However, an employment agreement can protect the local government if the manager resigns by specifying the amount of notice that must be given in order to allow the city or county to find a replacement. An employment agreement also usually includes a provision for payment in the event that the manager is fired for reasons that don't involve illegal or improper behavior (common severance agreements provide the manager six months' pay to ensure that he or she has a source of income while searching for another position).

The ICMA has created a Model Employment Agreement that is available for download on its website.[3] The major components of the model agreement include the following:

1. Term. What length of time does the agreement cover?

2. Duties and authority. What are the manager's legal and professional responsibilities under the agreement?

3. Compensation. What is the base pay? What is the schedule for payments, bonuses, and adjustments to compensation?

4. Health, disability, and life insurance. What will the employer pay for and what will the employee be responsible for?

5. Vacation, sick, and military leave. How will the employee accrue vacation and sick leave and how will military service be handled?

6. Automobile. Will there be a car provided or a car allowance?

7. Retirement. What will the employer contribute toward a retirement plan? What is the employee expected to contribute and what are the options for making contributions?

8. General business expenses. Will the organization pay for the individual to be a member of professional associations? Will it pay for travel to national, state, and regional meetings and for continuing education? Will the organization provide or reimburse the employee for the use of mobile communication devices, laptops, or other technologies?

9. Termination. What are the conditions by which termination can occur, and what rights does the employee have?

---

3. See http://icma.org/en/icma/career_network/career_resources/model_employment_agreement.

10. Final payment. Will there be a package providing the employee all or a portion of his or her base pay for a specified period of time following termination?[4]

11. Resignation. What method and time frame are required when an employee resigns?

12. Performance evaluation. When and how will performance reviews occur?

13. Hours of work. What are the expectations for participating in activities outside the standard work week? What flexibility will be given to the employee to establish an appropriate work schedule?

14. Outside activities. What activities (voluntary or paid) would be seen as a conflict of interest for the employee?

15. Moving and relocation expenses. Are employees required to live within the boundaries of the jurisdiction? What will the employer pay to help the employee and his or her family relocate to the new community?

16. Home sale and purchase expense. Will the employee be reimbursed for costs associated with selling, building, or buying a home?

17. Indemnification. What legal protection will be provided to an employee carrying out the duties and responsibilities of the job?

18. Bonding. Will the employer bear the cost of bonds for the employee?

19. Other terms and conditions. What other provisions not covered in the employment agreement apply to the employee?[5]

20. Notice. How will the employer and employee be notified of the agreement?

21. General provisions. How can this agreement be amended, modified, or adjusted?

---

4. To be valid and enforceable in North Carolina, the final payment (similar to a severance package) needs to be deferred final compensation for past service and included in a written employment agreement. Leete v. Warren Cnty., 341 N.C. 116 (1995). A reasonable provision provides enough risk protection for a promising manager to accept the offer, especially if local politics are unstable. A final compensations agreement can keep a candidate from pursuing other jobs, especially when there are controversies or political splits on the board. In addition, a negotiated agreement often makes an eventual involuntary parting of the ways more professional and less adversarial.

5. Such provisions could include local acts and state laws and codes.

Valid employment agreements are binding on current and future boards. Even if the manager is terminated legally, it is likely that the provisions of the employment agreement will be enforceable. According to Ellis Hankins, Executive Director of the North Carolina League of Municipalities,

> Unless it is amended with consent of both parties or expires at a stated time, the agreement stays in force, and future governing boards must abide by its provisions. The agreement is a contract, enforced just like any other contract. A future board may decide that the manager cannot do the job as it wanted it done. Since the statutes provide that the manager serves at the pleasure of the council, the council can ask the manager to resign or terminate him (if issues cannot be worked out). The council cannot contract away that right.[6]

Early Employment Stage

A new manager will need some time to adapt and get to know the job. Particularly during the early stages of employment, it is important to set expectations for the manager and meet with him or her regularly to see how things are going. The manager's contract with the board should also delineate a probationary period during which either party may be released from the contract without penalty.

Probation

The length of probationary periods varies, but a six-month period is common. Even though North Carolina managers serve as at-will employees and can be terminated by the board at any time without cause, it is helpful to have a few months during which the new manager and board are aware that either can sever the relationship without penalty. It may be appropriate for the board to establish a different final compensation arrangement for someone who is dismissed during the probationary period as part of the manager's employment agreement.

Evaluation

At the end of the probationary period, the board should conduct an assessment to evaluate how successful the new manager has been in accomplishing short-term goals and developing positive relationships with employees, board members, people in the community, and

---

6. S. Ellis Hankins, "Reasonable Manager Employment Agreements Are a Good Idea," *Southern City* LIV, no. 1 (January 2004): 2.

other key stakeholders. After the initial assessment, the board should evaluate the manager at least yearly. During annual evaluations, board members have an opportunity to discuss the manager's performance, acknowledge his or her success in various areas, and identify ways in which the board can help make the manager's job easier. The evaluation also provides an opportunity for the board to suggest areas in which the manager could improve.

The Board–Manager Relationship

The manager works for the entire governing board, not just the mayor or board chair or a subcommittee. Therefore, the entire board needs to consider its relationship with the manager and ask whether it is doing its best to provide a quality working environment for the manager. If the board is making it difficult for the manager to do his or her job effectively, it may find itself going through the hiring process on a regular basis. The discussion questions below are designed to help a board establish and maintain its relationship with the manager.

I was employed and found out shortly after being hired that there was deep division . . . on a five-member board over the departure of the prior manager. It made the job very difficult and was not a pleasant experience.

Questions for Discussion

1. What are the board's expectations for the new manager during the first few months? What should be in the initial work plan?
2. What salary and benefits are we willing to offer?
3. What should be in the employment agreement or contract?
4. How long should the probationary period be?
5. How will the new manager's performance be evaluated? How often will the assessments be conducted?

Conclusion

The board's responsibility for hiring a professional manager is clearly established by law, but the process for hiring a manager is less clear. Because there are no set standards for hiring a city or county manager, each local governing board must decide what approach works best in its unique situation. To ensure that the new manager will be well suited for the job, the board needs to agree on expectations and design a process that will enable it to hire the best possible candidate.

A professional manager can provide quality services and continuity for governing boards, local governments, and communities. Getting the right fit today may be one of the board's most important investments in the future.

Not all expensive, good-looking shoes will hold up on a long hike. The best fit is the most important quality to seek.

Appendix 1: Eight Expectations for Effective Board–Manager Relations

Expectation 1: The Manager Is an Organization Capacity-Builder
- Manager implements and updates business practices and processes
- Manager effectively and efficiently employs management tools
- Manager attracts and retains talented and motivated personnel
- Manager ensures that county operations run smoothly and routinely

Expectation 2: The Manager Is a Valued Advisor to the Governing Board
- Manager offers balanced and impartial policy advice to the governing board
- Manager recommends any measures he or she deems expedient, including alternatives and relevant information on the different options
- Manager sometimes makes an unpopular recommendation that might not have very good prospects of being accepted
- Manager fully supports governing board decisions and ensures that the administration does the same
- Manager helps elected officials explain their decisions to the public and helps the public understand the governing board's point of view

Expectation 3: The Manager Strives Jointly with the Governing Board to Provide Good Service to Citizens
- Manager assertively ensures that administration provides the very best service possible to the community
- Manager creates an organizational culture of responsiveness and performance, both in providing routine services to citizens and in handling special requests and complaints
- Manager takes personal risks on behalf of employees and fully accepts responsibility with the governing board when things go wrong

- Manager gives governing board members the necessary information to follow up with citizens if they wish

- Manager supports citizens and steers their complaints to administration

- Manager encourages governing board members to inform the manager of problems and give him or her the opportunity to solve them

Expectation 4: Elected Officials' Relationships with Employees Are Carefully Managed

- Governing board members observe the chain of command

- Governing board members and manager protect planned workflow

- Manager allows direct contact between governing board members and employees for routine inquiries or requests as long as these requests do not affect administrative workloads

- Governing board members submit substantial requests to the entire governing board and the board decides whether to take action

Expectation 5: The Governing Board Acts as a Body and Is Dealt with as a Body

- Governing board members take official actions as a body

- Manager welcomes suggestions from individual governing board members that do not conflict with policy

- Individual governing board members' requests that set new directions or require resource reallocations are put before the entire body

- Manager treats all governing board members alike ○

- Manager seeks to prevent governing board members from being surprised or caught off guard on issues

- Manager ensures all governing board members have the same level of information and understanding

Expectation 6: The Manager and the Governing Board Give Each Other a Chance to Prove Themselves

- Manager directs administration based on what a majority of the governing board decides

- Manager expects newly elected officials to give manager a chance to prove that he or she can serve the new members

- Governing board members recognize and accept that campaign rhetoric seldom stands up to the complexity of governing, leading, or managing
- Manager seeks to earn the trust and the confidence of new board members

Expectation 7: The Manager and the Governing Board Freely Give and Seek Feedback

- Manager and governing board members work to maintain open communications
- Manager provides all governing board members with accurate, relevant, and timely information
- Governing board members ask questions and make their interests, positions, and feelings known to the manager
- Governing board members offer constructive criticism to the manager on an ongoing basis
- Governing board members clarify their expectations of the manager and provide direction and benchmarks for success
- Governing board members and manager freely give and accept feedback in the spirit of continuous improvement

Expectation 8: The Manager and the Governing Board Work Together to Develop a Highly Effective Team

- Manager prepares agendas and plans meetings that focus on major topics
- Manager coaches governing board chair and members in developing high-performing habits such as
  - Thinking and acting strategically and with a vision for the community's future
  - Respecting the "shared constituency" with the citizens who also have relationships with and are served by other local and state governments
  - Demonstrating teamwork
  - Mastering small-group decision making
  - Honoring the board–staff partnership
  - Allocating governing board time and energy appropriately in four key areas: goal-setting retreats, study sessions, regular public hearings and meetings, and community relations
  - Having clear rules and procedures for governing board meetings
  - Obtaining objective feedback and conducting systematic and valid assessments of policy and implementation performance
  - Practicing continuous personal learning and leadership development

- Manager and board chairs orient new governing board members, encouraging new members to do their homework, ask good questions, and exercise caution and courtesy when speaking publicly about the county and staff
- Manager and governing board members behave in a manner that encourages citizen confidence in county government

Appendix 2: Practices for Effective Local Government Management

From *The Effective Local Government Manager, Third Edition* (pp 237–239), © copyright 2004 International City/County Management Association, Washington, DC. Adapted by permission of the publisher.

Note: When administering and scoring this exercise, it is important to take into account the positions of the participants. Varied roles in the organization will lead to varied responses.

Instructions for participants:
1. Read through the nineteen practices below.
2. Mark whether you think the management practice is highly important (H), moderately important (M), or unimportant (L) for your local government.
3. List your six most important (H) and six least important (L) practices.

Instructions for the board:
1. Tally the top priorities for the entire board to see where there are areas of agreement and disagreement on what practices are most important for your local government.
2. Once you have identified a set of priority practices, these can be used in developing a job advertisement and questions for candidates during the interview process.

Six Most Important Practices	Six Least Important Practices

1. STAFF EFFECTIVENESS: Promoting the development and performance of staff and employees throughout the organization (requires knowledge of interpersonal relations; skill in motivation techniques; ability to identify others' strengths and weaknesses). The following practices contribute to staff effectiveness:

- *Coaching/mentoring.* Providing direction, support, and feedback to enable others to meet their full potential (requires knowledge of feedback techniques; ability to assess performance and identify others' developmental needs).
- *Team leadership.* Facilitating teamwork (requires knowledge of team relations; ability to direct and coordinate group efforts; skill in leadership techniques).
- *Empowerment.* Creating a work environment that encourages responsibility and decision making at all organizational levels (requires skill in sharing authority and removing barriers to creativity).
- *Delegation.* Assigning responsibility to others (requires skill in defining expectations, providing direction and support, and evaluating results).

2. POLICY FACILITATION: Helping elected officials and other community actors identify, work toward, and achieve common goals and objectives (requires knowledge of group dynamics and political behavior; skill in communication, facilitation, and consensus-building techniques; ability to engage others in identifying issues and outcomes). The following practices contribute to policy facilitation:

- *Facilitative leadership.* Building cooperation and consensus among and within diverse groups by helping them identify common goals and act effectively to achieve them; recognizing interdependent relationships and multiple causes of community issues and anticipating the consequences of policy decisions (requires knowledge of community actors and their interrelationships).
- *Facilitating board effectiveness.* Helping elected officials develop a policy agenda that can be implemented effectively and that serves the best interests of the community (requires knowledge of role/authority relationships between elected and appointed officials; skill in responsibly following the lead of others when appropriate; ability to communicate sound information and recommendations).
- *Mediation/negotiation.* Acting as a neutral party in the resolution of policy disputes (requires knowledge of mediation/negotiation principles; skill in mediation/negotiation techniques).

3. FUNCTIONAL AND OPERATIONAL EXPERTISE AND PLANNING (a component of Service Delivery Management):

The following practices contribute to functional and operational planning and expertise:

- *Functional/operational expertise.* Understanding the basic principles of service delivery in functional areas—for example, public safety, community and economic development, human and social services, administrative services, public works (requires knowledge of service areas and delivery options).
- *Operational planning.* Anticipating future needs, organizing work operations, and establishing timetables for work units or projects (requires knowledge of technological advances and changing standards; skill in identifying and understanding trends; skill in predicting the impact of service delivery decisions).

4. CITIZEN SERVICE (a component of Service Delivery Management): Determining citizen needs and providing responsive, equitable services to the community (requires skill in assessing community needs and allocating resources; knowledge of information gathering techniques).

5. PERFORMANCE MEASUREMENT/MANAGEMENT AND QUALITY ASSURANCE (a component of Service Delivery Management): Maintaining a consistently high level of quality in staff work, operational procedures, and service delivery (requires knowledge of organizational processes; ability to facilitate organizational improvements; ability to set performance/productivity standards and objectives and measure results).

6. INITIATIVE, RISK TAKING, VISION, CREATIVITY, AND INNOVATION (a component of Strategic Leadership): Setting an example that urges the organization and the community toward experimentation, change, creative problem solving, and prompt action (requires knowledge of personal leadership style; skill in visioning, shifting perspectives, and identifying options; ability to create an environment that encourages initiative and innovation). The following practices contribute to initiative, risk taking, vision, creativity, and innovation:

- *Initiative and risk taking.* Demonstrating a personal orientation toward action and accepting responsibility for the results; resisting the status quo, and removing stumbling blocks that delay progress toward goals and objectives.
- *Vision.* Conceptualizing an ideal future state and communicating it to the organization and the community.

- *Creativity and innovation.* Developing new ideas or practices; applying existing ideas and practices to new situations.

7. TECHNOLOGICAL LITERACY (a component of Strategic Leadership): Demonstrating an understanding of information technology and ensuring that it is incorporated appropriately in plans to improve service delivery, information sharing, organizational communication, and citizen access (requires knowledge of technological options and their application).

8. DEMOCRATIC ADVOCACY AND CITIZEN PARTICIPATION: Demonstrating a commitment to democratic principles by respecting elected officials, community interest groups, and the decision making process; educating citizens about local government; and acquiring knowledge of the social, economic, and political history of the community (requires knowledge of democratic principles, political processes, and local government law; skill in group dynamics, communication, and facilitation; ability to appreciate and work with diverse individuals and groups and to follow the community's lead in the democratic process). The following practices contribute to democratic advocacy and citizen participation:

- *Democratic advocacy.* Fostering the values and integrity of representative government and local democracy through action and example; ensuring the effective participation of local government in the intergovernmental system (requires knowledge of and skill in intergovernmental relations).
- *Citizen participation.* Recognizing the right of citizens to influence local decisions and promoting active citizen involvement in local governance.

9. DIVERSITY: Understanding and valuing the differences among individuals and fostering these values throughout the organization and the community.

10. BUDGETING: Preparing and administering the budget (requires knowledge of budgeting principles and practices, revenue sources, projection techniques, and financial control systems; skill in communicating financial information).

11. FINANCIAL ANALYSIS: Interpreting financial information to assess the short-term and long-term fiscal condition of the community, determine the cost-effectiveness of programs, and compare alternative strategies (requires knowledge of analytical techniques and skill in applying them).

12. HUMAN RESOURCES MANAGEMENT: Ensuring that the policies and procedures for employee hiring, promotion, performance appraisal, and discipline are equitable, legal, and current; ensuring that human resources are adequate to accomplish programmatic objectives (requires knowledge of personnel practices and employee relations law; ability to project workforce needs).

13. STRATEGIC PLANNING: Positioning the organization and the community for events and circumstances that are anticipated in the future (requires knowledge of long-range and strategic planning techniques; skill in identifying trends that will affect the community; ability to analyze and facilitate policy choices that will benefit the community in the long run).

14. ADVOCACY AND INTERPERSONAL COMMUNICATION: Facilitating the flow of ideas, information, and understanding between and among individuals; advocating effectively in the community's interest (requires knowledge of interpersonal and group communication principles; skill in listening, speaking, and writing; ability to persuade without diminishing the views of others). The following practices contribute to advocacy and interpersonal communication:

- *Advocacy.* Communicating personal support for policies, programs, or ideals that serve the best interests of the community.
- *Interpersonal communication.* Exchanging verbal and nonverbal messages with others in a way that demonstrates respect for the individual and furthers organizational and community objectives (requires ability to receive verbal and nonverbal cues; skill in selecting the most effective communication method for each interchange).

15. PRESENTATION SKILLS: Conveying ideas or information effectively to others (requires knowledge of presentation techniques and options; ability to match presentation to audience).

16. MEDIA RELATIONS: Communicating information to the media in a way that increases public understanding of local government issues and activities and builds a positive relationship with the press (requires knowledge of media operations and objectives).

17. INTEGRITY: Demonstrating fairness, honesty, and ethical and legal awareness in personal and professional relationships and activities (requires knowledge of business and personal ethics; ability to understand issues of ethics and integrity in specific situations). The following practices contribute to integrity:

- *Personal integrity.* Demonstrating accountability for personal actions; conducting personal relationships and activities fairly and honestly.
- *Professional integrity.* Conducting professional relationships and activities fairly, honestly, legally, and in conformance with the ICMA Code of Ethics (requires knowledge of administrative ethics and specifically the ICMA Code of Ethics).
- *Organizational integrity.* Fostering ethical behavior throughout the organization through personal example, management practices, and training (requires knowledge of administrative ethics; ability to instill accountability into operations; and ability to communicate ethical standards and guidelines to others).

18. PERSONAL DEVELOPMENT: Demonstrating a commitment to a balanced life through ongoing self-renewal and development in order to increase personal capacity (includes maintaining personal health; living by core values; continuous learning and improvement; and creating interdependent relationships and respect for differences).

19. BOARD RELATIONS: Developing and maintaining quality relationships with each member of the governing board and with the board as a whole (requires skills in communication; clear understanding of roles and responsibilities; ability to create trust among the parties; willingness to freely give and receive information).

Appendix 3: Questions You May and May Not Ask During a Job Interview

Subject	You may ask . . .	You may not ask . . .
Name	What is your full name? Have you ever worked under a different name?	Is that a German surname (*or any national origin*)? Do you prefer to be called Dr., Mr., Mrs., or Ms.?
Residence	What is your address?	How long have you lived at that address? I see you lived in Mexico, were you born there? Who else lives with you? Do you own or rent your home?
Race, color, or ethnicity	*For record keeping purposes only, on a form kept separate from the application, you may ask,* What is your race or national origin?	Would you change your (hair, eye, skin tone) for this job?
Sex	*For record keeping purposes only, on a form kept separate from the application, you may ask,* What is your gender?	Are you pregnant? How much do you weigh? How tall are you? Would you submit a photo of yourself?
Age	Can you submit legal proof of age upon employment? Are you over 18 years old?	What year were you born? How old are you?
Marital and family status	Are you able to meet the work schedule for this position?	Are you married? Do you have children? Are you planning children? What are your child care arrangements?
Religion	Are you able to meet the work schedule for this position?	What church do you attend? What holidays do you observe?
Citizenship	Are you legally eligible to work in the United States?	In what country or countries do you hold citizenship? Were you born in the United States or are you a naturalized citizen? Were your parents born in the United States? Where was your spouse born? Where were you born?
Education	Where did you go to college or graduate school? What areas did you study? What degrees did you earn? What certificates or diplomas have you received?	Was that college affiliated with a religious institution? What was your grade point average? What was your class standing? What were the dates you were enrolled?

Subject	You may ask . . .	You may not ask . . .
Organization	Are you a member of any professional organizations or trade unions related to this work?	Are you a member of the local social club, charity league, fraternity, or lodge?
Health and physical characteristics	Can you perform the essential duties of this job with or without reasonable accommodation?	Are you in good health? How did you get that scar? How tall are you? How much do you weigh?
Financial status	What are your salary requirements?	What is your credit score? Are your wages garnished? What debt do you have? Do you have any financial assets such as stocks, property, or an inheritance?
Arrest, conviction, and court record	Have you been convicted of any work-related crime?	Have you ever been arrested for any reason?
References	Who are your personal or professional references? Who referred you to us?	What is the name of your pastor or religious leader?
Military status	In which arm or branch of the military did you serve? When were you discharged? What was your rank, training, and experience related to this position?	Did you receive an honorable discharge? During what dates did you serve?
Type of job sought	What specific position are you looking for? Are you able to meet the work schedule?	Have you ever done ___? (*unrelated to the job*)
Experience	What is your work experience? Where were you employed? Who employed you? When did you work there? What position did you hold? Why did you leave that position? What has been your salary history?	What did you do at ___? (*unrelated to the job*)
Emergency contact	What is the name and contact information of the person we should call in case of emergency?	What is the name and contact information of the nearest relative to contact in case of emergency?
Non-job-related conduct	*Nothing*	What do you like to do in your free time? What kind of music do you like? Where do you like to go on vacation? (*or anything unrelated to the job*)

Adapted from James A. Buford Jr. and James R. Lindner, *Human Resource Management in Local Government* (Cincinnati: South-Western Publishing, 2002), 192–93. This resource provides excellent guidelines for pre-employment inquiries. It is adapted here to provide examples of actual questions that may and may not be asked.